BY LUCILLE RECHT PENNER

EATING THE PLATES
A Pilgrim Book of Food and Manners

THE COLONIAL COOKBOOK

THE HONEY BOOK

THE THANKSGIVING BOOK

THE FIRST THANKSGIVING

Celebration

THE STORY OF AMERICAN HOLIDAYS

Lucille Recht Penner

ILLUSTRATED BY Ib Ohlsson

Macmillan Publishing Company   New York
Maxwell Macmillan Canada   Toronto
Maxwell Macmillan International   New York   Oxford   Singapore   Sydney

To David, Zinaida, Yakov,
and Alexander Krimberg,
and to Beyla Rabinovich

—L.R.P.

This one's for Torben

—I.O.

Library of Congress Cataloging-in-Publication Data
Penner, Lucille Recht. Celebration : the story of American holidays / by Lucille Recht Penner ; illustrated by Ib Ohlsson. —1st ed.   p.   cm. Summary: Presents the origins and history of thirteen holidays, such as Columbus Day, Veterans Day, and Halloween. Also includes songs, maps, speeches, handicraft, and recipes. ISBN 0-02-770903-5
1. Holidays—United States—Juvenile literature.   [1. Holidays.]   I. Ohlsson, Ib, date. ill.   II. Title. GT4803.P46   1993
394.2′6973—dc20   92-25871

CONTENTS

1. HOLY DAYS AND HEROES   7

2. COLUMBUS DAY   10

3. INDEPENDENCE DAY   15

4. GEORGE WASHINGTON'S BIRTHDAY   22

5. ABRAHAM LINCOLN'S BIRTHDAY   28

6. MEMORIAL DAY   35

7. LABOR DAY   40

8. VETERANS DAY   44

9. MARTIN LUTHER KING DAY   49

10. NEW YEAR'S DAY   53

11. VALENTINE'S DAY   59

12. HALLOWEEN   63

13. THANKSGIVING DAY   69

14. CHRISTMAS DAY   74

1

HOLY DAYS AND HEROES

*. . . young and old
come forth to play
on a sunshine holiday.*

—*John Milton,*
L'Allegro

Hurrah!

It's a holiday!

Everyone loves a holiday. It's a time to have fun.

And it's even more fun if you know the stories behind the holidays. Every holiday has one. They are told in this book.

Some of our holidays celebrate highlights and heroes of American history. Others continue traditions that began long, long before the United States was born.

In ancient times, most holidays were religious. In fact, our word "holiday" comes from the words "holy day."

Primitive people worshiped the sun. The sun gave them warmth and light. It made their crops grow, so they had food to eat.

But in most parts of the world when winter came, the days got shorter, colder, and darker. Plants withered and died.

Would the sun ever return?

Yes! Some ancient people told the seasons from the stars. Others made calendars out of stones. They watched them carefully. They could tell from the stones' shadows when the days began to grow longer.

This meant that there would be a new season of crops. Life would continue! It was time to celebrate! People left their work. They gathered together to feast, to pray, and to thank the gods.

NEW YEAR'S DAY, HALLOWEEN, THANKSGIVING DAY, and parts of the CHRISTMAS DAY celebration can be traced back to these early holidays. VALENTINE'S DAY comes from an ancient Roman celebration. When we celebrate them we are continuing traditions that are thousands of years old.

Our newer holidays, those that began in America, help tell the story of our country's beginning and growth.

The story begins with an Italian explorer named Christopher Columbus. In 1492, Columbus sailed across strange seas and brought back news of a new continent—America. We honor him on COLUMBUS DAY.

In Europe, there was great excitement about America. Eventually, many Europeans sailed to America to live. The kings of European countries tried to claim America, saying it belonged to them.

But in 1776, American colonists fought a war against Britain to become a free, independent country. We celebrate the birth of this country every year on July 4th—INDEPENDENCE DAY.

We honor two great and beloved American presidents—George Washington and Abraham Lincoln—on PRESIDENT'S DAY.

While Abraham Lincoln was president, a bloody war—the Civil War—was fought between the Northern and Southern states. After the war, MEMORIAL DAY was proclaimed to honor the soldiers who died in battle.

On LABOR DAY, we honor another group of Americans—our working people.

VETERANS DAY is rooted in respect for members of the United States armed forces who fought around the world.

The story of the American struggle for freedom comes full circle with the celebration of the birthday of a man dedicated to justice, equality, and peace—MARTIN LUTHER KING, JR.

American holidays are celebrated with flags, parades, and picnics. It's fun!

When we celebrate these special American holidays we are celebrating our country, our ancestors, and the ideals we live by.

2
COLUMBUS DAY

(second Monday in October)

In fourteen hundred
And ninety-two
Columbus sailed
The ocean blue.

—*old rhyme*

Christopher Columbus was a brave Italian explorer and a great navigator.

In 1492, Columbus and his crew, in three tiny ships, left the coast of Spain and sailed into the unknown. They crossed a vast, uncharted ocean and arrived on the shores of a new world.

Columbus is often called the discoverer of America. But did he actually discover America?

No. Other people were here first. American Indians had settled in America thousands of years before Columbus.

Norsemen had explored the coast of North America five hundred years before Columbus arrived.

Still, most Europeans didn't know America existed when Colum-

NEW WORLD

bus set sail. Even Columbus didn't know. He was trying to sail somewhere else. He found America by accident!

Columbus thought he could sail straight from Europe to the Indies—India, China, Japan, and the Spice Islands of Indonesia. Others had dreamed of this before him. But he was the first to try to do it.

Caravans had already traveled eastward, overland from Europe, to the Indies. This was a long, exhausting, expensive trip. It often took years to get there and back.

But men who made the trip also made their fortunes. In the Indies, they traded for spices, precious jewels, silk, and gold. They sold these for huge profits when they returned home—*if* they returned. The trip was very dangerous, and many travelers died.

Columbus believed he could find an easier, faster, safer way to the Indies. He would travel not by land, but by sea—and not east, but west!

Could you visit a neighbor by walking *away* from his house, and going clear around the block, and coming to his house from the other side? Columbus had the same idea. He thought he could sail clear around the world and get to the Indies that way.

Most other seamen of his time were afraid to sail out of sight of land. But Columbus was a true adventurer. He was willing—eager, in fact—to be the first to attempt the unknown.

Who was this brave man?

How did he become one of the greatest explorers and navigators the world has ever known?

Christopher Columbus was born in the Italian seaport of Genoa. As a boy, he saw ships from foreign countries coming and going. Cargo of every kind was loaded and unloaded. It was exciting! Columbus longed to go to sea.

He sailed on his first voyage in 1476. Little by little, he studied maps and learned how to navigate. As his experience grew, he became a wise and clever sailor.

Columbus didn't know there were five oceans. He thought there was only one big one. People called it the "Ocean Sea." On the other side of it, he thought, were the Indies.

Columbus knew the world was round. But he didn't know how big it was! He thought he could sail across the ocean easily.

Still, such a voyage would be very expensive. He needed somebody rich to help pay for his trip. King Ferdinand and Queen Isabella of Spain agreed to give Columbus three ships—the *Niña*, the *Pinta*, and the *Santa Maria*. They also gave him money to hire sailors and to buy food and supplies.

Finally, on August 3, 1492, Columbus and his men set sail.

For weeks, all they saw were waves and sky, sky and waves. Columbus was excited, but his sailors began to get worried. No one had *ever* sailed so far from land.

Every day the wind blew from the east, pushing them farther and farther west. How would they ever be able to sail home against it? The men began to feel sure they would never get back.

But Columbus cried "Adelante," which means "Forward!"

So the sailors decided to kill Columbus. They planned to throw his body overboard, and then sail home. They would say he had died at sea.

Just in time, a lookout suddenly shouted, "Land!"

The men crowded the deck. It was true. They had come to an island near the coast of America. The native people were very friendly. They gave Columbus and his men fresh water to drink and sweet fruit to eat.

Although Columbus saw that people were living on the island, he claimed it for the king and queen of Spain. He even forced some Native Americans onto his ship and took them back to Spain. On later voyages he enslaved some of the native people.

In fact, Columbus's voyage to America was the first step in a painful clash between Europeans and Native Americans. As a result of their contact with Europeans, many Native Americans died of diseases like smallpox, to which they had no immunity. Others were driven from their homes by European settlers hungry for land and furs.

But to the people of his time Columbus was a hero. They were thrilled to see the spices, gold, tropical fruits, and beautiful red-and-gold parrots he brought back as presents for King Ferdinand and Queen Isabella.

Columbus sailed back and forth across the ocean three more times. At the end of his third voyage he was brought home in chains because his companions thought he had governed a new Spanish settlement, Santo Domingo, badly. But the queen sent Columbus on a fourth voyage to the New World.

Although Columbus was sure he had landed near China, he never actually found a route to the Indies. What he found for Europe was something even more important—the New World of America.

After Columbus's great voyages, other people gradually began to travel from Europe to America—to trade, to explore, and finally to settle.

Now, on Columbus Day, we remember his special place in American history.

3
INDEPENDENCE DAY

(July 4)

Give me liberty or give me death!
—*Patrick Henry, 1775*

Happy Birthday, America!

Almost three hundred years after Christopher Columbus sailed to America, a new country was born—the United States of America.

Who were the citizens of this new country?

The first people who followed Columbus across the ocean were adventurers. They came to hunt, fish, trade with the Indians, and search for gold. Then they went back home to Europe. They certainly did not want to remain in such a wild place.

By the 1600s, however, many English people and other Europeans had made America their home. They lived in thirteen colonies spread out along the eastern coast of North America.

The colonies were ruled by Britain and the people who lived in them paid taxes to the British king.

These taxes kept getting higher and higher!

In the 1700s, the colonists got angry. They had to pay taxes, but they couldn't help make the laws. All the laws were made far away in Britain.

It didn't seem fair. *No taxation without representation!* became a slogan of the angry colonists.

But the British didn't pay any attention. In fact, they demanded new taxes on molasses, tea, spices, and almost everything the colonists needed.

So the colonists decided to break away. They wanted to run their own country. Patrick Henry, a politician from Virginia, gave a speech. "Give me liberty or give me death!" he shouted. Everyone cheered.

Something had to be done. But no one wanted war. Maybe it would be possible to reason with the British.

Delegates from each of the colonies held a meeting. It was called the Continental Congress. The delegates agreed that they would not buy anything from Britain if Britain did not lower taxes.

Instead of lowering taxes, the British sent soldiers to America.

The Continental Congress met again. The delegates were furious. They decided the time had come to form an army and fight for their freedom.

A Declaration of Independence was adopted by the Congress on July 4, 1776, and sent to King George III. It stated that:

ALL PEOPLE ARE CREATED EQUAL.

ALL PEOPLE HAVE THE RIGHT TO LIFE, LIBERTY,
AND THE PURSUIT OF HAPPINESS.

A GOVERNMENT MUST PROTECT THESE RIGHTS FOR
ITS PEOPLE.

IF IT DOESN'T, THE PEOPLE HAVE THE RIGHT TO
OVERTHROW THEIR GOVERNMENT AND CREATE
A NEW ONE.

King George, according to the Declaration, had made unjust laws and demanded unfair taxes. For these reasons, the colonies were declaring themselves independent of Britain. They would form their own government. From now on, they would rule themselves!

Messengers carried copies of the Declaration throughout the colonies. In every town, the Declaration was read aloud from the steps of the church, or in the town square.

In some places, only a few people knew how to read. In one small town in South Carolina, the only person able to read the Declaration to the townspeople was a nine-year-old boy. His name was Andrew Jackson.

Some of the words were long and hard: *unalienable, usurpations, despotism.* But Andrew Jackson read the Declaration from beginning to end in a loud, clear voice. Many years later, when Andrew grew up, he became the seventh president of the United States.

The Declaration was also read aloud to the Continental Army, in New York City. The soldiers cheered. That night they pulled down a big lead statue of King George III, broke off its head, and melted the lead to make bullets.

The Revolutionary War had begun.

At first it seemed that the British were sure to win. They had the strongest army in the world. Most of the colonial soldiers were poorly fed and clothed. Many marched on bare feet. How could they ever win?

Fierce battles were fought. Victory went back and forth.

JULY 4, 1886

Then France decided to help the Americans. French warships blockaded the British army from the sea while Americans attacked it from land.

The British army finally surrendered. The war was over. At last, the colonies were independent! They chose a name for themselves: the United States of America.

The day on which the United States declared its independence from Britain—July 4th—became special to Americans. We celebrate it every year.

In some years, the July 4th celebration has been especially meaningful to our country.

On July 4, 1848 the cornerstone was laid for the George Washington Monument in Washington, D.C. A copy of the Declaration of Independence was buried under the monument.

July 4, 1876 was the one hundredth birthday of the Declaration. A Centennial Exposition was held in Philadelphia. (A hundredth birthday is called a "centennial.") A marvelous invention was introduced at the Exposition—the telephone, which Alexander Graham Bell had just invented.

The people of France presented a wonderful gift to the people of the United States on July 4, 1884. It was the Statue of Liberty. The statue holds a torch in her right hand and a book in her left. July 4, 1776 is carved on the cover of the book. Although the statue was actually unveiled on October 28, 1886, it was intended as a birthday present.

On July 4, 1898 the Spanish-American War ended when American ships defeated Spanish ships commanded by Admiral Pascual Cervera y Topete. The American admiral, William T. Sampson, wrote to President William McKinley, "The ship under my command offers the nation, as a Fourth of July present, the whole of Cervera's fleet."

No fireworks were allowed in coastal American cities on July 4, 1942. The United States was at war. The lights might help German or Japanese bombers find their targets. President Franklin Roosevelt said, "We celebrate it this year, not in the fireworks of make-believe, but in death-dealing reality of tanks and planes and guns and ships."

When Alaska became the forty-ninth state on July 4, 1959 a new star was added to the American flag.

Another new star was added to the flag on July 4, 1960 as Hawaii became the fiftieth state.

On July 4, 1976 America celebrated its bicentennial—its two hundredth birthday!

Each Fourth of July, the red, white, and blue American flag still waves its fifty stars proudly throughout the United States of America.

YANKEE DOODLE

The British soldiers had better clothing and supplies than the colonists. They teased the ragged Americans by singing a song called "Yankee Doodle."

The British jeered and sang "Yankee Doodle" before a famous battle at Concord, Massachusetts. But the Americans won the battle!

After that, "Yankee Doodle" became an American song. It is often sung on the Fourth of July.

4

GEORGE WASHINGTON'S BIRTHDAY

(February 22)

First in war, first in peace,
and first in the hearts of his countrymen.

—*Light-Horse Harry Lee*

Make way for the king of the United States of America!
What?

Of course we don't have a king. But when the United States won
independence from Britain, some Americans did want to choose a
king.

They asked a man everyone knew and loved—George Washington—to be the first king of the United States.

But Washington said no. He didn't think the United States should
have a king. So instead of choosing him as king, the people elected
George Washington as the first president of the United States.

Many people consider him the greatest of American heroes. In

WASHINGTON'S RAGTAG ARMY

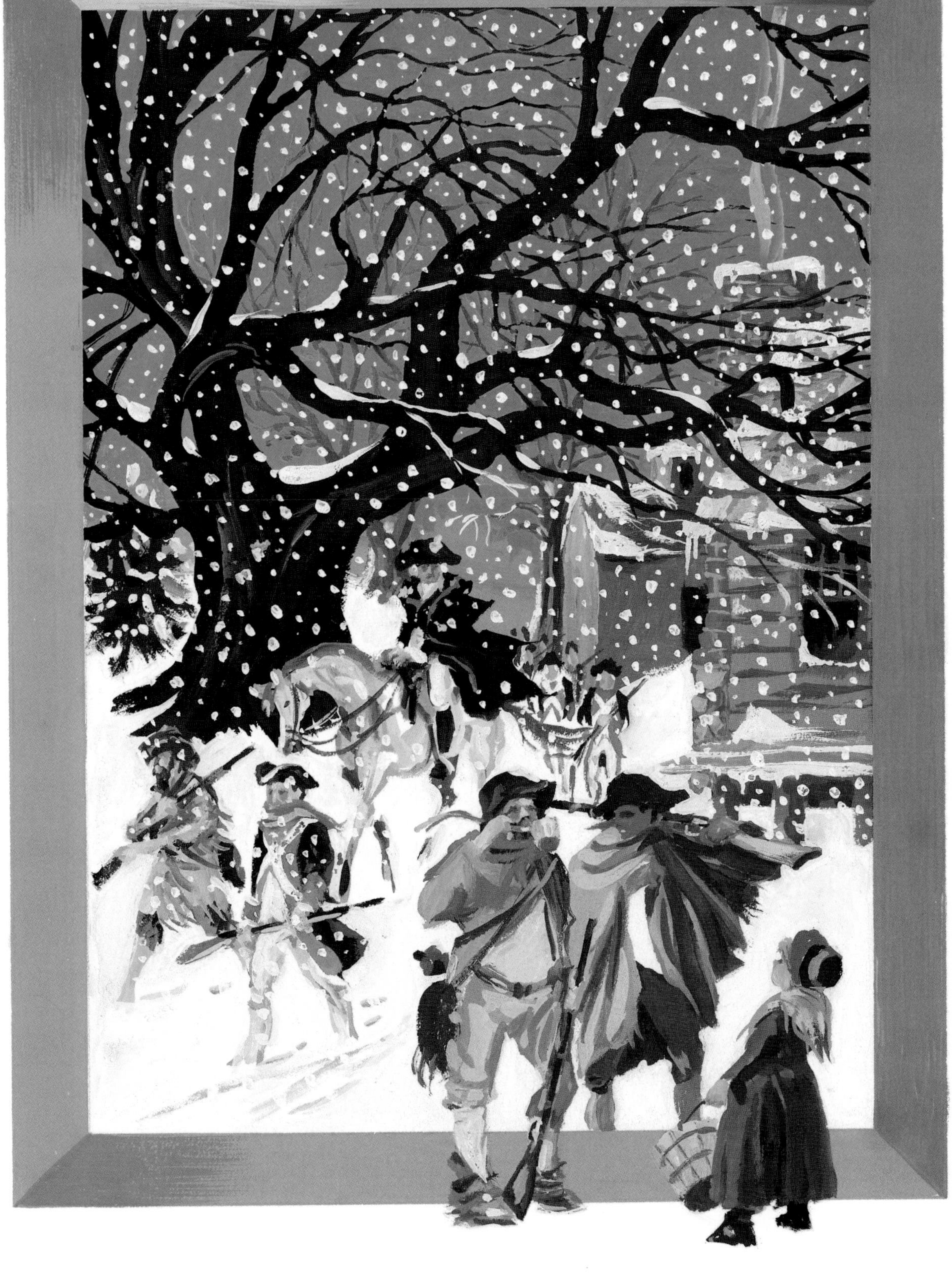

fact, he was so important to the creation of the United States that he is sometimes called the father of his country.

George Washington was born February 22, 1732, on a farm in Virginia.

As a boy and a young man, he was very strong and good at sports. He loved to hunt, fish, sail, row, dance, and ride horses.

Many stories were told about his great strength. It was said that he could bend a horseshoe with his bare hands! Once, he was supposed to have hurled a silver dollar clear across the broad Potomac River.

What did George Washington look like? We don't have any photographs of him. Photography wasn't invented until the 1830s. But many artists painted portraits of George Washington.

He was more than six feet tall and weighed over two hundred pounds—a huge man for the time in which he lived. He had reddish hair, blue eyes, and skin marked with smallpox scars.

He also had trouble with his teeth. In fact, Washington wore false teeth for most of his life. Some were made out of wood. Others were made from the teeth of cows, pigs, and elk. Some were even made from hippopotamus ivory. All the teeth looked funny and felt uncomfortable. Washington rarely smiled.

His first love was the sea. But his mother wouldn't let him become a sailor. She was afraid he would be drowned.

Instead he became a surveyor. He helped to measure and make maps of new farms and towns. His understanding of geography would prove very useful in later years when he was a military commander.

When Washington was twenty-one, he enlisted in the Virginia militia. As an ally of the British, he fought against the French and

Indians. Washington liked being a soldier. After his first battle he wrote, "I heard the bullets whistle, and believe me, there is something charming in the sound."

When the Revolutionary War broke out, George Washington's fellow colonists asked him to serve as their commander in chief.

Leading the Continental Army was a hard job. Soldiers enlisted for only a few months. When their time was up they might walk off immediately—even if an important battle was planned for the next day. Sometimes a hundred men left at once.

Other men deserted the army even before their time was up. Many of them were farmers. They had to go home and harvest their crops. Besides, they were lonesome for their families. They didn't think of themselves as professional soldiers.

The men who remained almost never had enough blankets, food, or clothing. Washington's army was described as "more than half naked and two-thirds starved."

But Washington was a clever general. He knew the weaknesses of the British army.

British soldiers carried packs weighing more than one hundred pounds. They had to carry them even into battle.

And British soldiers wore tight, itchy, wool uniforms—even in summer. Their tall bearskin hats had no brims, so the sun glared into their eyes.

It was exhausting and uncomfortable to be a British soldier. The British army moved *very* slowly.

Washington taught his soldiers to strike and then retreat quickly.

The British were amazed. They thought war should be fought according to their rules. Everyone should stand still and shoot off their guns. When enough people on one side were killed or wounded, then the other side could advance.

Washington didn't fight by British rules. And his tiny army won the war. At last he could return home to his wife and family. His work was done.

Or so he thought. In 1789, an election was held for president of the new United States of America. George Washington got twice as many votes as any of the other candidates. So he was called back to public service.

At his inauguration, Washington showed his country's independence by making sure that everything he wore—his clothes, his shoes, even his sword—had been made in the United States.

He served as president of the United States for two terms—a total of eight years.

George Washington died at his beautiful home, called Mount Vernon, in 1799, when he was sixty-seven years old. Everyone was sad. Many people wore black clothes to show their grief. A vault was built for Washington under the dome of the Capitol building in Washington, D.C., but he is actually buried at Mount Vernon.

Americans can never forget George Washington. Our nation's capital—Washington, D.C.—is named after him, and so is the state of Washington.

In his honor, the world's tallest obelisk—555 feet high—was built in Washington, D.C. This is the Washington Monument. Millions of people visit it every year.

And George Washington has monuments of another kind. Nuts from a large black walnut tree that grows at Mount Vernon have been planted all over the country by Boy Scouts.

George Washington was so well loved that people all over the United States began celebrating his birthday while he was still alive!

In 1790, the first year that Washington was president, Congress adjourned on his birthday and sent him congratulations. In later years, Washington's birthday was often a time for parades, parties, and patriotic speeches.

In 1961, President John F. Kennedy said in a speech that "the spirit of George Washington is a living tradition, so that even today he serves his country well."

Many states celebrate a special holiday on the third Monday in February. This holiday honors George Washington, Abraham Lincoln, and all our other presidents. It is called President's Day.

MOUNT VERNON

George Washington lived on a large plantation in Virginia called Mount Vernon. It covered almost eight thousand acres. There he grew tobacco, wheat, and corn. He also raised cattle.

His house was a large, white building overlooking the Potomac River. Today it is a national shrine. Many of the rooms still contain the furniture and dishes that George Washington and his family actually used. The pictures that he looked at every day still hang on the walls. The bed in which Washington died still stands in his bedroom.

Every year thousands of people visit George Washington's house, walk through its gardens, and rest under the large trees that were planted by Washington himself more than two hundred years ago.

5

ABRAHAM LINCOLN'S BIRTHDAY

(February 12)

Abraham Lincoln, his hand and pen,
He will be good, but God knows when.

—*ditty written by Abraham Lincoln*

Many people think that Abraham Lincoln, our sixteenth president, ranks alongside George Washington as the greatest of Americans. There is an old saying that Washington founded our country—and Lincoln saved it.

Abraham Lincoln was born on February 12, 1809, ten years after Washington died. In 1865, he was shot and killed by an assassin.

A special train carried Lincoln's body from Washington, D.C., to his burial place in Illinois. Thousands of people waited silently next to the railroad tracks. Many wept as the funeral train passed slowly by.

Yes, Abraham Lincoln was greatly loved.

But he was also greatly hated. In his day, the country was bitterly

28

divided over two great issues. One was "Union." The other was the slavery issue.

"Union" meant that the United States was one country. It must not be split up. Lincoln believed strongly in Union. So did most people in the Northern states.

But some Southern states wanted to secede—to drop out of the United States. These Southern states joined together and called themselves the Confederacy. They elected their own leaders and even printed their own money.

Many Southerners also wanted to continue the practice of slavery. Slave labor made it possible for them to operate huge tobacco and cotton plantations.

Most Northerners had only small farms. They didn't need slaves, and they had come to feel that slavery was evil. Lincoln himself said, "As I would not be a *slave,* so I would not be a *master.* This expresses my idea of democracy."

Northerners and Southerners could not agree. Finally the people of South Carolina announced that they were seceding from the United States. Union forces marched against them.

The Civil War had begun.

It was our most terrible war. Often family members and friends had to fight against each other. Thousands of people who didn't die from battle wounds died of disease, hunger, and poverty caused by the war.

When the fighting finally ended, the Union forces had won. Much of the South was in ruins.

And on December 18, 1865, Congress passed the Thirteenth Amendment to the United States Constitution. It abolished slavery in the United States forever.

Millions of Americans thought that President Lincoln had made

the world a better place. Some called him "Father Abraham" to show their love. But others hated him and cursed his name.

Who was Abraham Lincoln? How did he find the strength and the courage to work so hard for the things he believed were right?

Abraham Lincoln was born on a small farm in Kentucky. His family was poor, and the children had to work hard. There wasn't even time for Abraham to go to school. He said later that all his schooling added up to only one year.

Though neither of his parents could read or write, Lincoln taught himself how to do so by reading the only book in the house—the Bible—over and over and over.

He also taught himself arithmetic by writing problems on a wooden board. After he wrote the answers, he scraped off the writing with his knife, and then wrote new problems.

As he grew older, Lincoln began to borrow books from neighbors. If he heard that someone had a book, he would walk miles to borrow it. He read by firelight, after his chores were done.

Lincoln was a tall boy, and he grew into an extremely tall and powerful man. He wrote this description of himself:

> I am in height six feet four inches, nearly; lean in flesh, weighing, on an average, one hundred and eighty pounds; dark complexion, with coarse black hair and gray eyes.

He worked at many different jobs. He was a soldier and a shop-keeper. He held the position of postmaster, sometimes keeping the letters in his hat. Like George Washington, he worked as a surveyor. Finally he became a lawyer.

Lincoln was elected to the Illinois state legislature and then to the

United States Congress. In 1860, he was elected president of the United States.

It was the hardest time to be president. The Civil War raged during his two terms in office. And although he worked desperately to keep the country together, President Lincoln never got to enjoy the resulting peace.

On April 14, 1865, a few days after the war had ended, Lincoln and his wife were attending a play at a theater in Washington.

Suddenly John Wilkes Booth—an actor who had supported the Southern cause—leaped into the president's box and shot Lincoln through the head.

Lincoln died the next day. He was fifty-six years old.

The whole nation was shocked and saddened. The following year, on February 12—Lincoln's birthday—a memorial service was held in Washington, D.C. Hundreds of mourners sobbed as Andrew Johnson, the new president of the United States, paid tribute to the fallen leader.

In 1892, Illinois made February 12 a state holiday in honor of Lincoln. Soon many other states did the same.

On February 12, 1905, a special memorial service was held in Kentucky. President Theodore Roosevelt made a speech and laid the cornerstone of a marble shell that was being built to cover the log cabin in which Lincoln had been born.

And on February 12, 1915, the cornerstone was laid for the Lincoln Memorial in Washington, D.C. The memorial is a beautiful marble building containing a huge statue of Lincoln, as well as tablets inscribed with two of his most moving speeches—his second Inaugural Address and the Emancipation Proclamation. More than two million people visit the Lincoln Memorial every year.

Many towns, rivers, bridges, schools, and highways are named

THE GETTYSBURG ADDRESS

During the Civil War, a fierce battle was fought between the Northern and Southern armies at Gettysburg, Pennsylvania. Almost forty thousand soldiers were killed in three days!

Four months later, President Lincoln gave this speech at a ceremony to dedicate part of the battlefield as a cemetery for the soldiers who had died in the terrible battle.

Four score and seven years ago our fathers brought forth on this continent, a new nation, conceived in Liberty, and dedicated to the proposition that all men are created equal.

Now we are engaged in a great civil war, testing whether that nation, or any nation so conceived and so dedicated, can long endure. We are met on a great battlefield of that war. We have come to dedicate a portion of that field, as a final resting place for those who here gave their lives that that nation might live. It is altogether fitting and proper that we should do this.

But, in a larger sense, we cannot dedicate—we cannot consecrate—we cannot hallow—this ground. The brave men, living and dead, who struggled here, have consecrated it, far beyond our poor power to add or detract. The world will little note, nor long remember what we say here, but it can never forget what they did here. It is for us the living, rather, to be dedicated here to the unfinished work which they who fought here have thus far so nobly advanced. It is rather for us to be here dedicated to the great task remaining before us—that from these honored dead we take increased devotion to that cause for which they gave the last full measure of devotion—that we here highly resolve that these dead shall not have died in vain—that this nation, under God, shall have a new birth of freedom—and that government of the people, by the people, for the people, shall not perish from the earth.

after Abraham Lincoln. His familiar face is printed on the five-dollar bill and engraved on the penny. Americans will never forget him.

Many people believe that if Lincoln had not been president, the Union would have lost the Civil War. The United States would have been divided into two countries. And slavery might have lasted many years more.

When we celebrate Lincoln's birthday, we also celebrate democracy, freedom, and justice in America.

6
MEMORIAL DAY

(last Monday in May)

Soldier, rest! thy warfare o'er.
   Sleep the sleep that knows not breaking,
Dream of battled fields no more,
   Days of danger, nights of waking.

—*Sir Walter Scott,*
The Lady of the Lake

A memorial is a tribute to people who have died. And Memorial Day began as a way of honoring soldiers who had died in the American Civil War.

When the Civil War ended in 1865, President Lincoln wanted to welcome the Southern states back to the Union. "With malice toward none; with charity for all," he said, "let us strive . . . to bind up the nation's wounds."

But after Lincoln was killed, people were not charitable. It was hard for them to forgive their enemies or to forget the terrible suffering caused by the war.

More Americans died in the Civil War than in any other American war before or since. Most families had at least one relative who was killed. Soldiers were so sure they were going to die that many wrote their names on scraps of paper and pinned them to their uniforms before each battle. That way their dead bodies could be easily identified.

When the war ended, there was great mourning for those who had died. Many memorial services were held throughout the United States. At least twenty towns and cities claim to have held the original Memorial Day.

One of the first ceremonies was held on May 5, 1866, in Waterloo, New York. A Joint Resolution of Congress recognizes Waterloo as "The Birthplace of Memorial Day."

The people of Waterloo marked the day by closing their businesses and stores. They flew their American flags at half-mast, a sign of mourning. Then they went to the cemetery and decorated soldiers' graves with flowers, ribbons, and flags.

Two years later, in 1868, General John Alexander Logan chose May 30 as the special day to honor Union soldiers who had died in the Civil War. He suggested the name "Decoration Day." It would be a day, he said, for "strewing with flowers or otherwise decorating the graves of comrades who died in defense of their country."

General Logan also helped to start an association of Union veterans of the Civil War. It was called the Grand Army of the Republic, and it organized Decoration Day celebrations every year until most Civil War veterans had died. Then the national veterans' organization—the American Legion—took over. The holiday came to be called Memorial Day.

Southern states organized special holidays—such as Confederate Memorial Day and Confederate Heroes Day—to honor Confederate soldiers who had died in the Civil War.

In 1971, a law was passed making Memorial Day a federal holiday in the United States. Both Union and Confederate soldiers who died in the Civil War are honored. So are soldiers who died in the Spanish-American War, the First World War, the Second World War, the Korean War, the Vietnam War, and the Persian Gulf War.

Since the end of the First World War, Poppy Day has also been celebrated on Memorial Day.

Poppies, beautiful red flowers, came to symbolize death after the First World War. During that war, many American soldiers fought in Europe. In the spring, red poppies flowered on European battlefields where thousands of soldiers had fallen and died.

On Poppy Day, veterans' organizations sell real and artificial poppies. They donate the money they collect to help disabled veterans.

POPPIES

Would you like to make poppies to wear and give to your friends on Memorial Day?

It's easy to do. You will need only a few supplies:

red crepe paper
green pipe cleaners

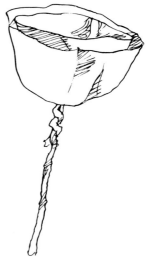

Cut out two four-inch circles of crepe paper for each poppy. Put one circle over the other.

Make two holes in the center, going through both circles. Put the end of a pipe cleaner up through one hole, bend it, and bring it down through the other. Twist to tie. The long end of the pipe cleaner is the stem. You can put it in your buttonhole.

Smooth the crepe paper "petals" of the poppy.

MEMORIAL DAY (MAY 5, 1866)

How is Memorial Day celebrated today? Most of all, by parades! Boy Scouts, Girl Scouts, and veterans' groups march and ride in floats.

Often the Gettysburg Address, the moving speech that President Abraham Lincoln delivered during the Civil War, is recited at memorial services.

In memory of the dead, flags are flown at half-mast on public buildings and on navy ships. Tiny boats filled with flowers are set afloat at major ports to honor sailors of the United States Navy who have died at sea.

Special services are held at Arlington National Cemetery in Arlington, Virginia, and at other military cemeteries around the United States. A bugle player plays "Taps," slowly and sadly, over the dead soldiers' graves.

Memorial Day is a day of remembrance and of gratitude.

7
LABOR DAY

(first Monday in September)

> *I've been working on the railroad*
> *All the livelong day.*
> *I've been working on the railroad*
> *Just to pass the time away.*
>
> —*old folk song*

On Memorial Day, we honor soldiers who died for our country, and on Labor Day we honor another special group of Americans—working people.

In the 1600s, immigrants began arriving in America from Europe. Immigrants are people who come to live in a new country.

It took the first immigrants weeks to cross the ocean in dark, stuffy, crowded sailing ships. But in the 1870s, sailing ships were replaced by steamships. Now the trip took only ten days.

And more and more immigrants came—many millions of them. They came to work in mines, mills, and factories all across the United States.

The immigrants often found working conditions that were horrible. So, in the 1800s, they began to organize themselves into unions.

Bricklayers got together. Carpenters did too. Each group of workers formed a union. Then some of the unions banded together to form an even bigger group. They called themselves the Knights of Labor.

In 1882, one labor union in New York City decided to organize a Labor Festival. They would have a picnic and a parade. It would be the first time a holiday was held just for American workers.

Some union leaders wondered if anyone would come. Wouldn't most people be afraid of losing their jobs if they took a day off to go to the Labor Festival?

But the organizers chose a date for the Festival—September 5, 1882—and notified all the unions in the city.

At ten-thirty on the morning of the great day, only the grand marshal of the parade and a few organizers showed up. They looked around sadly. Wasn't anyone else coming?

Then they heard music.

The jewelry workers union had come with its own brass band!

Soon the bricklayers arrived. They had made a float. It was a horse-drawn carriage holding a little building with brick walls and steps. And *they* had also brought a brass band.

Now more and more workers arrived. Some were wearing work clothes. They carried signs:

FAIR PAY!
SHORTER HOURS!
STOP CHILD LABOR!
SAFE WORKING CONDITIONS!

Soon there were ten thousand workers marching down the street. They all marched to a nearby park. The leaders made speeches.

41

The bands played. People sang, danced, and set off firecrackers.

The next day, news of the parade was reported in newspapers all over the United States.

Workers everywhere wanted to do the same thing. The idea of Labor Day caught on quickly. Towns and cities planned parades and picnics. Soon annual celebrations were being held in every state. On June 28, 1894, Congress proclaimed Labor Day to be a federal holiday.

A holiday in honor of the American worker had been born!

Hard work and low pay.

That's not fair!

In the 1700s and 1800s, many people had to work fourteen, fifteen, or sixteen hours a day. Some of them were children!

Hungry children would work for almost nothing.

Where did they work? Some children worked underground in dark mines. Because they were smaller than adults, they could fit in lower tunnels and narrower shafts.

Other children worked in hot, filthy factories and mills. Often they operated dangerous machinery. And sometimes they were tied to their machines so they couldn't run away.

Most child workers never went to school or got enough food or sleep. In Labor Day parades, union members held up signs—STOP CHILD LABOR!—to get people's attention.

Finally, laws were passed to protect child workers. Now children have to be at least fourteen years old to work. They can't work long hours or do dangerous jobs. And children have to get fair pay for the work they do.

8
VETERANS DAY

(November 11)

When Johnny comes marching home again,
Hurrah, hurrah!
We'll give him a hearty welcome then,
Hurrah, hurrah!
The men will cheer and the boys will shout,
The ladies they will all turn out,
And we'll all feel joy when Johnny comes marching home.

—Patrick S. Gilmore,
When Johnny Comes Marching Home

Labor Day honors American workers—and some of the hardest-working Americans are members of the armed forces. The special day for honoring them is Veterans Day.

Veterans Day was originally called Armistice Day. An armistice is a truce—an agreement to stop fighting between countries that are at war.

President Woodrow Wilson proclaimed the first Armistice Day in 1919. It celebrated the signing of the armistice ending the First World War.

The First World War was fought between two groups of countries. Britain, France, Russia, Belgium, Serbia, and the United States were called the Allies. Their enemies were the Central Powers—Germany, Austria-Hungary, and the Ottoman Empire, which is now Turkey.

The war began in Europe. At first, the United States tried to stay out of it.

But the Germans did several things that made Americans angry. In 1915, a German submarine torpedoed the *Lusitania*—a passenger ship that was sailing from America to England. Almost two thousand men, women, and children died when the ship sank.

Then a secret telegram from the German government to the German ambassador in Mexico was intercepted and published in American newspapers. This telegram ordered the German ambassador to ask Mexico to attack the United States. In return, Germany promised that if it won the war it would give Mexico the American states of New Mexico, Arizona, and Texas.

A few months later, German submarines torpedoed two American navy ships. The sailors on board were killed.

President Wilson had tried hard to keep the United States out of the war. But he finally decided that Americans must fight in order to "make the world safe for democracy."

On April 5, 1917, the United States declared war on the Central Powers.

American troops landed in France later that year. As the first troops set foot on the beach, an officer shouted, "Lafayette, we are here!" He meant that America would now repay a favor that was more than one hundred years old. During the American war for independence, the Marquis de Lafayette—a French nobleman—had helped the Americans fight the British. Now Americans would help France fight the Germans.

Two years after the United States entered the war, the Allies finally won. Representatives of the warring countries signed an armistice.

What a joyous day! The whole world was glad when the guns stopped firing.

But eight-and-a-half million soldiers had been killed. Twenty million had been wounded. Countless civilians had died of hunger and disease. Homes, businesses, and farms were destroyed.

The armistice was signed on November 11, 1918. And President Wilson named November 11 as Armistice Day. He urged Americans to spend the day celebrating the end of the war and remembering the suffering it had caused.

In 1938, Armistice Day was made an official federal holiday.

People everywhere had hoped that the First World War would be the "war to end all wars." But in 1939, the Second World War began. More than sixteen million soldiers died in the Second World War. The fighting didn't end until 1945.

In 1954, President Dwight D. Eisenhower—who had been a general in the Second World War—asked Congress to change the name of Armistice Day to Veterans Day. Now veterans of *all* American wars are honored on Veterans Day.

People celebrate the day by hanging American flags outside their houses. Communities hold parades in which veterans march and military bands play music. Spectators line the streets, waving flags and applauding the marching soldiers.

THE VIETNAM WAR MEMORIAL

On Veterans Day, 1982, a special memorial in Washington, D.C., was dedicated to soldiers who had fought and died in the Vietnam War.

It was called the Vietnam War Memorial.

The memorial is a huge wall of polished black granite. The names of all the men and women in the American armed forces who fought and died in Vietnam—almost sixty thousand of them—are chiseled into the wall.

The dedication of the memorial began with a parade and speeches. Thousands of Vietnam veterans came. Some were in wheelchairs. They searched the wall for the names of their dead friends.

People cried. They reached out and touched the names carved into the black stone. Husbands, wives, parents, and children of dead soldiers placed letters and flowers near the wall.

This Veterans Day was a special day of remembrance, grief, love, and honor.

9
MARTIN LUTHER KING DAY

(third Monday in January)

Free at last,
free at last,
thank God Almighty,
I'm free at last!

—Words from spir-
itual carved on the
gravestone of Martin
Luther King, Jr.

Veterans Day honors men of war. Martin Luther King Day honors a man of peace.

Martin Luther King, Jr., was born in Atlanta, Georgia, on January 15, 1929. When he was a child, many places in the United States were segregated by law.

Segregation meant that white and black people had to stay apart. Black children like Martin couldn't go to school with white children. Black people couldn't eat in the same restaurants as whites, or drink from the same drinking fountains. They had to sit in the back of public buses.

When he grew up, Martin became a minister. He preached in a church. And he worked for equality for black people. He wanted them to have the same civil rights as everyone else in the United States.

Civil rights include freedom of speech, the right to own property, the right to vote, and the right to receive equal treatment from the government.

Segregation laws meant that people weren't treated equally. These laws weren't fair. But they had been around for a long time. People were used to them. How could King help change their minds?

Sometimes people try to change things by fighting. King wanted to change things peacefully. He said blacks should go into "white" restaurants, drink from "white" water fountains, and sit in the front of the bus. But they shouldn't fight. If the police came, they should let themselves be arrested and go quietly to jail.

King said again and again: Don't obey unfair laws. But don't fight back!

Many people were furious at him for trying to change things. Some even wanted to hurt or kill him. He was stabbed in New York. He was stoned in Chicago. But he was brave. And his ideas for peaceful change worked.

He began by helping to organize a boycott of the buses in Montgomery, Alabama. All the black people should stay off the buses, he said, until they were allowed to sit in whichever seats they wanted. They shouldn't fight. They shouldn't hurt anybody. They just shouldn't ride the buses anymore.

The boycott worked. The Montgomery bus company lost a lot of money. The company agreed to let blacks sit anywhere they wanted.

King traveled all over the United States. He preached desegregation and equal rights. People listened to him.

Segregation

Finally, in 1964, the Civil Rights Act was passed by Congress. The Civil Rights Act makes it illegal to discriminate against anyone because of race, national origin, religion, or sex. And in the same year, King was awarded the Nobel peace prize "for leading the black struggle for equality through nonviolent means."

Four years later—on April 4, 1968—an escaped convict named James Earl Ray shot and killed King in Memphis, Tennessee.

His death was a shock to the whole country. Many people wanted to honor him. In 1984 Congress passed a law creating a new federal holiday—Martin Luther King Day—to be celebrated on the third Monday in January.

This special day is a good time to think about the life and work of Martin Luther King, Jr., and of the work still to be done to bring about his dream of justice for everyone.

"I HAVE A DREAM"

In 1963, Martin Luther King, Jr., led a march from the Washington Monument to the Lincoln Memorial in Washington, D.C. Two hundred and fifty thousand people marched behind him!

King gave a moving speech. He said, "I have a dream that one day this nation shall rise up and live out the true meaning of its creed: 'We hold these truths to be self-evident, that all men are created equal.'"

He was quoting famous lines from the Declaration of Independence:

We hold these truths to be self-evident, that all men are created equal, that they are endowed by their creator with certain unalienable Rights, that among these are Life, Liberty, and the pursuit of Happiness.

The work that Martin Luther King, Jr., did helped to change unjust laws and promote equality in the United States of America.

10

NEW YEAR'S DAY

(January 1)

Ring out the old, ring in the new,
  Ring, happy bells, across the snow;
  The year is going, let him go;
Ring out the false, ring in the true.

—Alfred, Lord Tennyson,
                    In Memoriam

Martin Luther King Day is the newest American holiday. New Year's Day—the first day of the year—is probably the oldest holiday in the world.

More than four thousand years ago, the ancient Babylonians were celebrating the start of each new year.

In 46 B.C., the Roman ruler Julius Caesar proclaimed January 1 as New Year's Day. On that day, Romans feasted and gave each other presents. They also gave New Year's gifts to their emperor. After a few years, Roman emperors began *demanding* gifts from their subjects on the first day of each year.

The Roman army conquered many countries, and Roman customs

NEW YEAR'S DAY

followed. English kings and queens adopted Roman practice by requiring New Year's gifts from *their* subjects. For instance, Queen Elizabeth I loved gloves. She received hundreds of pairs of jeweled and embroidered gloves as New Year's presents.

Another old New Year's custom is making as much noise as possible. In ancient times, people made noise at the start of the year in order to scare away evil spirits. In the 1700s, American colonists celebrated New Year's Day by shouting, cheering, and firing their muskets in the air. And at New Year's parties today, noisemakers are still part of the fun.

George Washington began a custom of holding a huge party on New Year's Day. It was an "open house." Everyone who wanted to attend was welcome. Today many families still hold open houses on New Year's Day.

Lots of people make New Year's resolutions. These are promises to do good things, or *not* to do bad things. Some people make resolutions to improve themselves: "I will go on a diet," or "I won't bite my nails this year." Other people resolve to help make the world a better place: "I will collect food for the homeless," or "I won't waste natural resources."

In some parts of the United States, people observe special New Year's customs. The Pennsylvania Dutch like to eat sauerkraut on New Year's Day. According to an old belief, this brings luck and wealth.

In the South, a special dish called Hopping John is served on New Year's Day. It's made by cooking black-eyed peas and rice. Eating Hopping John on New Year's Day is supposed to bring good luck. Sometimes children hop around the table before sitting down to eat their peas.

In San Francisco, office workers tear out their old calendar pages

HOPPING JOHN

1 cup dried black-eyed peas
¼ pound salt pork
1 cup white rice
½ teaspoon salt
¼ teaspoon pepper

Rinse the peas in cold water. Put them in a large pot. Add enough cold water to cover the peas.

Cover the pot and soak the peas overnight. In the morning, drain the peas.

Chop the salt pork. Put the pork and the peas in a six-quart saucepan with a tightly fitting lid. Add enough cold water to come just to the top of the peas.

Bring to a boil. Next, turn the heat to low. Cover the pot and simmer until the peas are tender, about 30 minutes. Some water will be left in the pot.

While the peas simmer, cook the rice according to the instructions on the package.

When the peas are tender, add the rice, salt, and pepper. Cover the pot. Simmer over very low heat until all the water is absorbed, about 15 minutes.

—Serves 8

Note: Ask an adult to help you chop the salt pork, and to pour and carry hot foods.

and throw them from the windows. The pages look like confetti drifting to the ground.

Many Americans go to football games or watch them on television. Parades are televised, too. Two huge New Year's parades are the Tournament of Roses and the Mummer's Parade.

The Tournament of Roses is held in Pasadena, California. Beautiful floats covered with fresh flowers are pulled by teams of horses.

The Mummer's parade in Philadelphia, Pennsylvania, is a fancy-dress parade. People dress up as wild animals or famous outlaws, like Robin Hood. Some just wear fancy costumes decorated with ribbons and streamers. They march to City Hall, where prizes are awarded for the best costumes.

New Year's Day is a happy time. It is a national and an international celebration.

And it is one that will be celebrated forever. Maybe some of the heroes we honor today will not always have holidays. Perhaps other people's birthdays will come to be honored instead. But as long as the earth revolves around the sun, people will be celebrating the start of the new year with gratitude and joy.

VALENTINE CARDS

II
VALENTINE'S DAY

(February 14)

Love somebody, yes I do,
Love somebody, yes I do,
Love somebody, yes I do,
Love somebody, but I won't say who.

—*old song*

Valentine's Day—like New Year's Day—was celebrated long before Columbus sailed to America. But it has become a beloved American holiday.

Valentine's Day isn't a legal holiday. Schools, banks, and stores stay open. Mail is delivered—lots of it! Millions of Valentine's Day cards—"valentines," for short—are sent all over the country.

No one knows exactly how Valentine's Day began.

It may have started in ancient Rome. Three thousand years ago, Rome was a small city. Hungry wolves lived right outside the city gates. They killed farm animals. Sometimes they even killed people.

The Romans prayed to Lupercus to keep them safe from wolves. Lupercus was the god of shepherds and their flocks. The Romans

59

held a festival for Lupercus every year on February 15. This festival was called the Lupercalia.

As the city of Rome grew larger, wolves were no longer a problem. But the Lupercalia was fun, and the Romans kept it. They changed it into a holiday for Juno, the Roman goddess of love and marriage.

On Juno's day, young Roman girls wrote their names on pieces of parchment and dropped them into a large urn. Boys lined up to pull the names out. When a boy pulled out a girl's name, she became his partner for the holiday. They played games and danced together. Sometimes they fell in love and married.

Later, the Lupercalia—now the holiday of Juno—became mixed together with the Christian holiday of Saint Valentine, which was also held in February.

Who was Saint Valentine? Nobody knows for sure.

One story says that he was a Christian priest who lived in Rome long ago. The emperor at that time, Claudius II, was having trouble getting soldiers for his army. Young men preferred to stay home with their wives.

Claudius figured out that the wives were the problem. So he said that no more young men could get married! But Valentine helped young people marry secretly. The emperor was angry and had Valentine put in jail.

The children of Rome, who loved Valentine, were very sad when he was put in jail. They wrote little notes and pushed them through the bars of his cell. The notes said they loved and missed him. These notes may have been the first valentines!

Later, Pope Gelasius I—the head of the Church—named February 14 the feast day of Saint Valentine. As the Christian religion spread, so did Saint Valentine's Day. It became a day for the expression of love. The English poet Geoffrey Chaucer wrote that even birds choose their mates on Saint Valentine's Day.

In America, Valentine's Day wasn't an important holiday until the time of the Civil War. Then it became wildly popular. Soldiers sent thousands of valentines to their wives and sweethearts.

At first, valentines were all made by hand. Starting in the late 1800s, machine-made valentines started to be sold in stores.

There were many different kinds.

Some valentines had little mirrors pasted in the center.

Other valentines were made like puzzles. The person who got the valentine had to figure out the message.

Mechanical valentines had strings to pull. When you pulled the string, the valentine waved its hand—or, sometimes, stuck out its tongue!

Most valentine cards are loving or funny. Often they are decorated with pictures of hearts. Hearts have stood for love since earliest times.

Every year, thousands of people have their valentines mailed from Loveland, Colorado. The postmaster there stamps each envelope "Loveland" with red ink.

Millions of valentines are sent all over the United States every year.

Schoolchildren send them to their classmates and teachers.

Children and parents send them to each other.

Sweethearts send them.

Husbands and wives send them.

Some are bought in stores. Some are handmade. But they all say something wonderful.

They say, "I love you."

A REBUS VALENTINE

A rebus valentine has a message in which pictures are substituted for some of the words. You can copy the one below or make up your own.

Cut a heart out of red colored paper. Write the message with felt-tip markers or a glitter pen.

I love you very much. Be my valentine.

12
HALLOWEEN

(October 31)

Trick or treat,
Smell my feet,
Give me something
Good to eat.

—*Halloween chant*

Everyone looks forward to Valentine's Day. Another holiday that children look forward to each year is Halloween.

Halloween is a scary and a joyous holiday.

How can it be both?

On Halloween, kids dress up as witches, ghosts, goblins, and other characters. They tell scary stories. But dressing up is fun! So are eating treats, bobbing for apples, and carrying jack-o'-lanterns.

Halloween traditions probably started in Britain and Ireland, more than two thousand years ago, during the Celtic New Year's Eve.

For the Celts, New Year's Eve fell on October 31. It was not a

63

happy occasion. The Celts were afraid of the coming winter. They thought evil spirits were chasing away the sun.

The most evil spirit of all was Samhain—the god of death. The Celts believed that Samhain came back to earth on the night of October 31. Goblins and the ghosts of the dead came with him.

Everyone was terrified. To hide themselves from the evil spirits, people wore costumes made out of animal heads and skins. Big bonfires were set alight. Crops, animals, and sometimes even people were burned in the fires as gifts to Samhain.

After the Romans conquered Britain in A.D. 43, the Samhain ceremonies got mixed up with two Roman festivals that also were held in October.

One, called the Feralia, honored the dead. The other honored Pomona, the Roman goddess of fruit. Her favorite fruit was thought to be the apple.

How did these three observances—the Samhain ceremony, the Feralia, and the Pomona festival—become Halloween?

In the ninth century, a Christian holy day called All Saints' Day was held on November 1. It was a day of celebration for all the saints and martyrs of the Church.

The night before All Saints' Day became known as "All Hallows' E'en." A *hallow* meant a holy person. *E'en* stood for evening. As time passed, All Hallows' E'en became shortened into one word—Halloween.

Back then, it was a *very* scary time. People really believed in witches. Witches who flew through the sky on their broomsticks. Witches who cast evil spells on people. Witches who had weird pets: black cats, spiders, toads, and bats.

To protect their homes from witches, people hung lucky charms on their doors. When they had to be outside at night, they made bonfires and carried torches to scare the witches away.

Today, children like to dress up on Halloween in black capes, witches' hats, and other costumes. They carry spiders, bats, and toads made out of paper or plastic. Then they go out trick-or-treating.

Trick-or-treating comes from an old Irish custom. Beggars used to go to the houses of rich people on October 31 and ask for gifts. They said the gifts were for Muck Olla—a god who was said to destroy the house of anyone who wasn't generous. So rich people usually gave the requested gifts. They were afraid of Muck Olla. They were also afraid of the beggars.

Today, children wearing costumes go from house to house. "Trick or treat?" they ask. It's almost always a treat—candy, apples, raisins, popcorn, or coins.

Often people set out jack-o'-lanterns on their doorsteps to welcome the trick or treaters. Jack-o'-lanterns are pumpkins with faces carved out of them. A candle or a flashlight is put inside the pumpkin at night. The faces glow in the dark.

An old Irish story explains that jack-o'-lanterns are named for a man called Jack. Jack was a miser, so when he died he wasn't allowed into heaven. But he had played jokes on the devil, so he wasn't allowed into hell, either.

Instead, Jack had to walk the earth forever. He had only a little lantern to light his way. And that is why he came to be called jack-o'-lantern.

How did Halloween reach the United States?
Halloween was brought to America mostly by people from Ireland. Millions of Irish came here in the 1800s when there were famines

in Ireland. They brought their Halloween customs with them.

Halloween spread rapidly across America. Soon almost everybody wanted to join in. Today, children all over our country wear costumes and go trick-or-treating on October 31. Halloween is a holiday every child looks forward to.

If the ancient Celts could see our Halloween, they might at first think we were still celebrating their old festival of Samhain.

They would see people disguised in strange costumes. Food would be set out for these strange creatures. Witches, goblins, and ghosts would be everywhere.

But one important thing would be different. Everyone would be having fun!

HALLOWEEN

BOBBING FOR APPLES

Fill a large metal tub with water. Put in one apple for each player.
Two or three people can bob for apples at the same time.

Here's how you do it:

      Kneel next to the tub.

      Put your hands behind your back.

      Try to grab an apple with your mouth.

      No hands allowed!

The first person to pull an apple out of the tub with his or her mouth
is the winner.

Be prepared for lots of splashing and laughing.

13
THANKSGIVING DAY

(fourth Thursday in November)

The Old Wives' Program
for Thanksgiving Week:

MONDAY—Wash
TUESDAY—Scour
WEDNESDAY—Bake
THURSDAY—Devour

—*Mother Goose*

Like Halloween, Thanksgiving combines ancient and modern customs.

To the first farmers, the fact that plants grew from seeds seemed like a miracle. Each year they thanked the gods for making a harvest possible.

In ancient China, a thanksgiving festival celebrated the birthday of the moon. In ancient Egypt, farmers pretended to weep with regret as they harvested their crops. They didn't want the spirits of the plants to be angry.

Native Hawaiians held a yearly Thanksgiving festival. It lasted four

THANKSGIVING DAY PARADE

months! Everyone feasted, played games, and brought gifts of food, flowers, and feathers to the altar of Lono, the god of plenty.

In England, a boy and girl sometimes were crowned king and queen of the harvest. They rode home from the fields in a cart filled with grain and decorated with flowers.

Thanksgiving in America began when a group of English settlers— the Pilgrims—arrived in 1620.

Would they have any harvest at all? Or would they starve?

Luckily, the Pilgrims made friends with the Indians who lived nearby. A Patuxet Indian named Squanto—who had learned English when he was kidnapped by an English sea captain years before— was their interpreter.

Squanto taught the Pilgrims how to plant Indian corn. Their first harvest was huge. The Pilgrims ground the kernels into meal—a kind of coarse flour. There was enough to last all winter.

When all their crops were gathered in, the Pilgrims held a harvest celebration. This was the first American Thanksgiving. The Pilgrims prepared a feast of corn bread, pudding, pumpkins, beans, squash, cod, bass, shellfish, and deer meat.

Did they also eat turkey? We can't be sure. One Pilgrim wrote in his diary that wildfowl was served. He might have meant duck or goose or turkey—or maybe all three.

The Thanksgiving celebration lasted for three days. This was the first time the Pilgrims had felt safe since they had set sail from England a year before. They had suffered terrible hardships and losses. Half of them had died. But the people who were left had built homes in the wilderness, signed a treaty of peace with the Indians, and raised enough food to be certain that they wouldn't starve.

For years after the Thanksgiving of 1621, there was no special day

A THANKSGIVING GAME

The Pilgrims invited an Indian chief named Massasoit to their Thanksgiving celebration. He came with ninety men. The Pilgrims and Indians showed off for each other.

The Pilgrims marched in formation, sounded their bugle and drums, and fired their muskets. The Indians shot at targets with bows and arrows. Everyone ran races and played games.

Here are directions for an old English game that may have been played at the Pilgrim Thanksgiving.

An Egg Race

Mark a starting line and a finish line on the ground. Have the runners stand at the starting line.

Give each one an uncooked egg to hold in a spoon.

Sound the signal to start.

The first person to cross the finish line with the (unbroken) egg in his or her spoon is the winner.

set aside for the holiday. Towns observed Thanksgiving whenever they felt like it, and whenever it was convenient.

It could be held early or late in the season. In 1705, the town of Colchester, Connecticut, put off its Thanksgiving celebration for several weeks because a ship bringing molasses had been delayed. People needed molasses to make pies and puddings.

It wasn't until 1863 that President Abraham Lincoln proclaimed a national Thanksgiving Day on the fourth Thursday in November. He said our blessings "should be solemnly, reverently, and gratefully acknowledged with one heart and one voice by the American people."

Every year after that, a thanksgiving holiday was officially proclaimed by the president. But it did not become a permanent holiday until 1941, when Congress passed a resolution officially establishing the holiday on the fourth Thursday in November.

On Thanksgiving, we often retell the story of the Pilgrim settlers. We feast on food they might have eaten more than three centuries ago—turkey, stuffing, sweet potatoes, corn, and pumpkin. It's a wonderful time to think about our immigrant heritage and the blessings of our present lives.

14
CHRISTMAS DAY

(December 25)

Christmas is a-coming,
The goose is getting fat,
Please to put a penny
In an old man's hat.
If you haven't got a penny,
A ha'penny will do.
If you haven't got a ha'penny,
God bless you!

—*old rhyme*

As soon as the last of the Thanksgiving turkey is eaten, many people begin counting the days until Christmas.

Christmas is one of the most popular American holidays. It's a Christian holiday, a celebration of the birth of Jesus Christ.

No one knows exactly what day Jesus was born. But his birthday is celebrated on December 25th. Christians believe he is the Son of God.

According to the Bible, a woman named Mary lived in the town of Nazareth in Palestine. One day an angel came to her. The angel

Everyone loves presents

told Mary that she would soon give birth to a child. Her child would be Jesus, the Son of God.

Mary and her husband, Joseph, traveled to the town of Bethlehem. When they arrived, the inn was crowded. The innkeeper let them sleep in the stable. That was where Jesus was born, in a manger.

Shepherds left their flocks in the fields and came to Bethlehem to see the baby. And three Magi—which means wise men—came from Persia to see the baby. They said they had followed a bright star in the sky all the way to Bethlehem.

The wise men and the shepherds worshiped Jesus. Almost two thousand years later, Christians still worship Jesus on Christmas Day.

In addition to celebrating the birth of Jesus, Christmas celebrations today include customs from long before the time of Jesus. For instance, the giving of gifts at Christmas is borrowed from an ancient Roman festival—the Saturnalia—which was held at about the same time of year. When the Romans became Christians, they gave up most of their Saturnalia. But they kept the gift-giving part, making it part of their Christmas holiday.

The first American settlers—the Pilgrims and Puritans—didn't like light-hearted holidays. They didn't approve of Valentine's Day or Halloween. And they didn't approve of Christmas.

In fact, in 1659 a law against Christmas was passed in Massachusetts. The law said that anyone caught celebrating Christmas would be fined!

But more and more immigrants kept coming to America, and many of them had loved Christmas in their own countries. Finally the laws against Christmas were changed. Today, Christmas Day is a federal holiday.

The first American Christmas card was printed in Boston in 1875. Today, millions of Americans send Christmas cards—often stamped with a special Christmas stamp—to their friends and families.

And millions of beautiful, green fir trees are sold at Christmas. People set them up in their homes and decorate them with cranberries, popcorn, painted wooden and glass balls, and little statues of angels. Before electricity was invented, candles were often tied on the branches. Now Christmas trees are lit with colored electric lights.

Each year a different state sends a Christmas tree to the White House on a huge truck. The president lights the tree in a special lighting ceremony.

Everyone loves giving and getting gifts! On the night before Christmas, presents are put under the tree. Children wake up early the next morning to open their presents.

The custom of Christmas gifts, which started with the Roman Saturnalia, is now associated with Santa Claus.

Who is Santa Claus? He's not a real person. The legend of Santa Claus is probably based on the story of Saint Nicholas.

Nicholas was a bishop who lived in Turkey long ago. He loved children and gave them many gifts. After he died, Nicholas was made a saint. His feast day became a major celebration in many countries.

The Dutch name for Saint Nicholas was *Sinterklaas*. It sounded like Santa Claus to English-speaking settlers in the United States.

There are many legends about Santa Claus. He is said to have a workshop at the North Pole where he and his helpers—Santa's elves—make toys for children. On Christmas Eve, Santa loads the toys into a sled. His reindeer pull the sled through the sky and land on the rooftops. Santa slides down the chimney of each house and puts toys under the Christmas tree.

There is even a town named Santa Claus in Indiana. Every year, people send thousands of Christmas cards to be mailed from there.

A SNOWFLAKE CHRISTMAS CARD

It's easy to make a beautiful Christmas card. All you need is:

red or green colored paper
white paper
scissors
paste
a felt-tip marker or a glitter pen

Fold the piece of colored paper in half.

Cut a circle four inches across out of the white
paper. Fold the circle in half, so it looks like this:

Then fold the half-circle in half. It will look like this:

Cut little shapes out of the middle of the folded paper, like this:
Don't cut the edges.

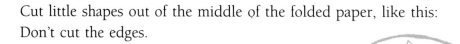

Open up the white paper. You will have a snowflake.
Paste it carefully onto the front of the folded piece
of colored paper.

Open up the card. Write "Merry Christmas"
inside with the felt-tip marker or glitter pen.
Sign your name at the bottom of the card.

That way, the cards get stamped with the postmark "Santa Claus."

Sending cards, giving and receiving gifts, decorating homes with Christmas trees, singing the songs of the season, and religious worship are all part of this beloved holiday. Most of all, Christmas is a time when everyone remembers these words:

PEACE ON EARTH, GOOD WILL TOWARD MEN.